P9-CDG-503

DISCARD

Vintage Paper Crafts

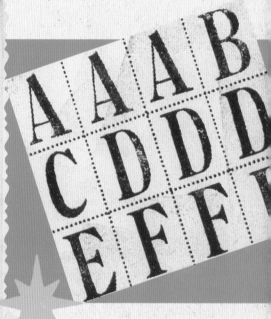

Anna Corba

Sterling Publishing Co., Inc. New York
A Sterling/Chapelle Book

Chapelle, Ltd.:
Jo Packham
Sara Toliver
Cindy Stoeckl

Editor: Lecia Monsen
Art Director: Karla Haberstich
Graphic Illustrator: Kim Taylor
Copy Editors: Anne Bruns, Marilyn Goff
Photography: Steve Aja Photography

Staff: Kelly Ashkettle, Areta Bingham, Donna Chambers,
Emily Frandsen, Lana Hall, Susan Jorgensen,
Jennifer Luman, Melissa Maynard, Barbara Milburn,
Suzy Skadburg, Kim Taylor, Linda Venditti, Desirée Wybrow

If you have any questions or comments, please contact:
Chapelle, Ltd., Inc., P.O. Box 9252, Ogden, UT 84409
(801) 621-2777 • (801) 621-2788 Fax
e-mail: chapelle@chapelleltd.com
web site: www.chapelleltd.com

The copy, photographs, instructions, illustrations, and designs in this volume
are intended for the personal use of the reader and may be reproduced for
that purpose only. Any other use, especially commercial use, is forbidden
under law without the written permission of the copyright holder.

Every effort has been made to ensure that all information in this book is
accurate. However, due to differing conditions, tools, and individual skills,
the publisher cannot be responsible for any injuries, losses, and/or other
damages which may result from the use of the information in this book.

This volume is meant to stimulate craft ideas. If readers are unfamiliar or not
proficient in a skill necessary to attempt a project, we urge that they refer to
an instructional book specifically addressing the required technique.

Library of Congress Cataloging-in-Publication Data

Corba, Anna.
Vintage paper crafts / Anna Corba.
p. cm.
Includes index.
ISBN 1-4027-1059-3
1. Paper work. I. Title.
TT870.C663 2004
745.54--dc22
2004000344

10 9 8 7 6 5 4 3 2 1

Published by Sterling Publishing Co., Inc.
387 Park Avenue South, New York, NY 10016
©2004 by Anna Corba
Distributed in Canada by Sterling Publishing
c/o Canadian Manda Group, One Atlantic Avenue, Suite 105
Toronto, Ontario, Canada M6K 3E7
Distributed in Great Britain by Chrysalis Books Group PLC,
The Chrysalis Building, Bramley Road, London W10 6SP, England
Distributed in Australia by Capricorn Link (Australia) Pty. Ltd.
P. O. Box 704, Windsor, NSW 2756, Australia
Printed and Bound in China
All Rights Reserved

Sterling ISBN 1-4027-1059-3

A FLOWER

Table of Contents

Meet Anna Corba . . . .

Date Inv. No. Entry No. Mark DESCRIPTION From Whom Steamer Item Cost Yen Commission

About Anna

I wasn't always drawn to the past. Growing up in the Midwest, I had an orange and lime bedroom filled with purple daisies which were definitely in step with the times. I even passed up my grandfather's Fiestaware without kicking myself until a few years later.

My love of worn objects began to unfold as I started to visit flea markets more out of necessity for affordable goods than anything else. This was before flea marketing became a national pastime. I immediately found comfort amidst the tarnished and torn; imperfections spoke to me of life really lived. I could be myself in this world, free to make mistakes and blunder along a bit haphazardly if need be. A chipped china cup or a torn valentine felt like a second cousin, and so I began to take them home.

Ji Stephonson   20
2 white shirts   20
2 Collard shirts   8
1 Flemel shirt   8
1 Night shirt   *paid*   2 3
9 Holchig   20
Socks marked F.S.

Date	Inv. No.	Entry No.	Mark		Drawn	DESCRIPTION	Duty	From Whom	Steamer	Item	Cost Yen	Commission

TRIUMPH

not able to nurse him, wait up
must pull up a little. She m
more care. That was why she
camp so early this afternoon.
home to rest. She had fai
at her work. So silly of he
self. Why, the war migh
and she must go on wor
just as Jim himself w
She must be worthy
more careful. She w
now, and after a
be fit again. She t
resumed on way,
but her chest was
hardly breathe.
thinking. She
somehow she w
had got round
through the
She looked a
strangely y
white.
After a

One of my first such treasures was a water-marked ledger from the late 1800s. It seemed extravagant to pay twenty dollars for someone else's accounting of lace and collars and rented rooms, but the handwriting was so beautifully formed in sepia ink, running just slightly where the water had seeped, that I couldn't just walk away. Thus began my true love of paper.

People standing next to me at sales will sometimes ask, "What do you collect?" I never have much of an answer for them. I don't look for anything specific, I just know "it" when I see it. That said, I do tend to gravitate to vintage sheet music, grade school grammar books, and all things French. I like pages yellowed with age and books with pencil notes in the margins.

11

Date   Inv. No.   Entry No.   Mark   ...Steamer   Item   Cost Yen   Comm

Pennsylvania R. R. Bridge over Conestoga Creek,
near Lancaster, Pa.

PER VIA AEREA
PAR AVION   Mod. 24-R

I don't worry about the provenance of things nor
do I worry about whether the manner in which I
reuse them will preserve them forever. I
think everything, even postcards and
soap labels have a natural life span and
my acquaintance with them is just one
step along the way.

Somewhere amidst this journey of
collecting photos, books, and assorted
whatnots, I began to feel a need to really
use these objects as opposed to just being
inspired by their beauty. Being a painter, I
began to include fragments of paper in my
mostly abstract compositions. Eventually
the fragments began to take over to a
point that my pieces became more about
collage than paint. This led to new acquisi-
tions and a wider array to choose from, and
before long I became consumed with the
idea of giving new life to these forgotten
pieces of the past. Laying aside the angst of
grappling with larger canvases, I now work
on smaller projects, many of which are
included in this book and can be accom-
plished in a matter of hours or days as
opposed to weeks. This allows me to utilize
my collections and gives me a perfect excuse
for adding to them frequently.

From Whom	Steamer	Item	Cost Yen	Commission

It is a joke in my family that we don't know where my creative gene came from; but I do know where my shopping gene came from and that is my mom. I find a certain lovely symmetry in the fact that many of my smaller projects have become part of my own product line which is sold in shops across the country where my mom can browse to her heart's content.

New ideas dance in my head constantly and the challenge of bringing them to fruition is very sustaining. I consider it a privilege to have been asked to share some of this world with you and I hope it serves to help your own inspirations unfold.

Anna

Date	Mark	Drayage	DESCRIPTION	Steamer	Item	Cost Yen	Commission

The Hunt

I am often asked, "Where do you find all your old stuff?" Well, you have to enjoy the hunt, as sources tend to be far and wide. Obvious choices are flea markets and secondhand stores. It is here that I find most of my "gems" including old photographs, botanical prints, bottles, and buttons. The key here is to keep visiting new venues, which is why traveling comes in handy.

I have stumbled across a book fair while lost in France, quickly scoured an antiques market unfurling its wares just as we were about to exit an Italian village, and hopped on the subway in New York to get to the 26th Street flea market during a heat wave in March.

I am not an early riser so you won't find me paying early bird entrance fees with a flashlight in my hand. Besides, I've discovered over the years that what I consider heart-palpitating treasure (even among kindred spirits) is not the same for others. I am frugal and I'm willing to dig. Odd-looking plastic bags and the dark recesses underneath tables have reaped fabulous rewards. For that matter, so have sidewalks. My husband often waits for me as I double back for bottle caps, patinaed metal scraps, shopping lists, and oversized paper clips.

I find some of my best old books, books that I feel I am rescuing by tearing them apart rather than damaging them, at library sales. I often go on the last day when paper grocery bags

are handed out to fill for a few dollars. Once again, it seems that there is always plenty of music, art, and foreign language left to choose from.

Our town has a wonderful thrift shop, run for charity, where I find lots of yellowed envelopes, parchment paper, and bags of old trim for pennies. This is also where I pick from games piled high on the shelves. Most are new but every now and again an old Scrabble or wooden domino set will appear.

Wandering the aisles of older hardware and stationery stores—the more crooked the wooden floor the better—is also quite fruitful. I am drawn to the humble yet utilitarian objects that are found here and love coming up with new applications for almost obsolete products: clothespins, cotton string, index cards, and obscure labels, all fit in this category.

I don't use the Internet although some friends call me nuts. A part of me doesn't want the search to be too easy. I find beauty and meaning in a process that requires a certain pounding-of-the-pavement commitment. I also value the ability to touch and hold that which I'm about to purchase.

Ephemera, stamp, and postcard shows are all valued resources. This is where I will find more expensive but truly worth it paper goods. I make certain I am on all these mailing lists and make friends with the dealers who most often have what I am looking for.

Of course, there is no discounting that one-in-a-million garage sale which yields the perfect vintage typewriter or gigantic spool of white cotton rickrack for under ten dollars.

Venture Forth Boldly!

Embellishment Suggestions

Oftentimes a lovely array of paper will be enough to create a wonderful project. Other times it's the little extra adornment that really defines a piece. For this reason there are certain items that I always try to keep on hand. They include wooden yardsticks which can be cut to various lengths to suit your needs, flattened bottle caps in a variety of colors—which can be hot-glued into place as an alternative to buttons—and wooden spools with or without thread. Vintage hats yield beautiful flowers, leaves, and velvet ribbons; and old lamp shades often have faded tassels that can be reworked either as tie-ons or glue-ons. I try to stay one step ahead of the game with my jars of buttons. I look for a wide assortment from kitschy (plastic and colorful) to the sublime (mother-of-pearl and decorative metal.) This way I am never left empty-handed.

I also look for cloth measuring tapes and funky old handkerchiefs, which can be used as a stand-in for ribbon to make whimsical floppy bows.

I don't think I've ever met a brass stencil or crystal chandelier drop that I didn't like. Both can be used as a wired-on or dangling element to a wall piece or journal spine.

Don't forget that displaying your collections is half the enchantment. I gather all sorts of jars with or without lids, glass pudding cups, enamel saucers, and muffin tins to provide easy organized access as well as to look inspirational lined up on shelves.

Some days I really can imagine these objects calling out "Look here, choose me!"

16

31

Date   Inv.

Cost Yen   Commission

très petit

Most Commonly Used Tools

Brayer
Chip brushes (disposable)
Clean cloth
Craft glue
Craft scissors
Decorative-edged scissors
Double-stick tape
Glue stick
Hole punch
Matte medium
Pinking shears
Rubber stamp images and
    alphabet with inkpads
Spray mount
Two-fluid-ounce bottles
    of acrylic paints
Wooden craft stick

General Tips

Beeswax

I often use beeswax as a final layer on collage projects in lieu of varnish. The wax mutes the colors and lends a soft warm depth that I find appealing. I am also drawn to the tactile quality of this medium. Heating it in my skillet, the aroma filling my studio, watching it drip from my brush, is my own little glimpse of alchemy.

My favorite wax is bleached beeswax, but it is not always easy to find. University art stores are usually your best bet or it can be ordered. Unbleached beeswax, either in crystals or blocks, can work; but it will leave a slight yellow cast. There are times when I simply use a creamy candle wax, which is easy to find at most craft stores. I mix this one-third wax to two-thirds paraffin. Otherwise it is just too soft to hold up. Its softness is fun to manipulate, however; so if you want lots of drips and character, go ahead and use this wax.

You will need to purchase an electric skillet with sides which you don't mind ruining. I have been lucky to find these at sidewalk sales or church rummage sales. If you are using blocks of wax, cut the blocks into 2" cubes. Melt your wax to 200° but do not heat over 200°. Have enough to fill your skillet at least ¼" deep. It also works to melt your wax in a bread pan, placed on the skillet. It takes slightly longer to melt, but it is an easy way to get a nice deep pool of wax.

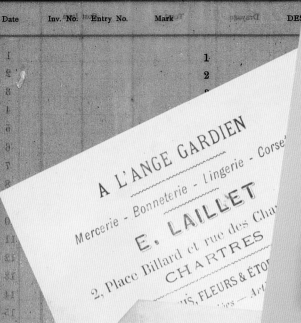

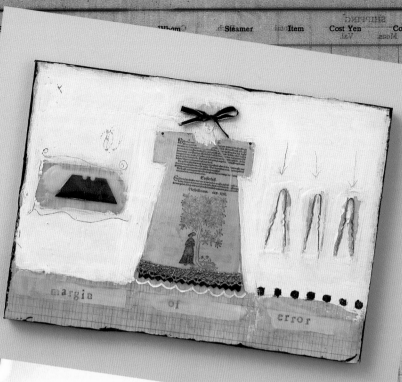

Lay your piece down flat on newsprint close to your skillet. Dip a chip brush, at least one-third as wide as your piece, in wax to saturate it, then quickly and evenly spread onto piece. Swipe your brush past the edges of your piece. Repeat strokes until surface is covered, overlapping the previous stroke slightly. The wax will dry quickly. I usually like the imperfections that occur in the surface; but if you would like a smoother look, you can achieve this by gently scraping with a razor blade.

It is fun to experiment with the wax. You can dip three-dimensional objects in it and they will be dry in a matter of moments. You can use it as an adhesive to add items to an already finished piece. Simply stroke the wax over your addition such as a paper scrap or postage stamp until it stays in place. I like drips to run down at this point.

When finished, simply unplug your skillet and allow the wax to cool and harden with your brushes right in it. This makes for easy storage and the brushes will soften back up when you reheat the wax. Scrape the bristles with a wooden craft stick to help keep them supple during the reheating process.

MANGEL

MAMA

Striped Paper

Painting your own paper to be cut up or torn creates an interesting way to really personalize your projects. I'll set aside an afternoon every now and again and create a nice stack to choose from over the next few months.

Tear a few pages out of a variety of books. By variety this means: white pages, yellowed pages, French text, Asian, text and so forth.

Lay pages out flat on newspaper. Choose paint colors that attract you. I have a variety of two-fluid-ounce bottles of acrylic paints that are found at any craft store. They are inexpensive so you can collect a nice palette.

Using a ¼" or ½" brush, dip generously in water, dab in color, and paint alternating stripes on several pages. I use a separate brush for each color so that I can work quickly. The key is to keep the paint transparent enough so that the text still shows through. Run your brush right off the edges of each page.

You can also paint polka dots scattered here and there on each page and fill in the background with another color. Loosely outline your dots with charcoal pencil for whimsical definition.

264

FIRST YEAR ITALIAN

Domande

1. Che è un treno omnibus? 2. Che è un treno rapido? 4. Dove vediamo gente in una grande stazione? 5. Sono tutti nella stazione perchè devono partire e perchè ritornano da un viaggio? 6. Quanti uffici ci sono nei treni italiani? 7. Che uffici ci sono in una grande stazione? 8. Di che sono carichi i facchini? 9. Che annunziano i segnali luminosi nella stazione? 10. Quanti posti ha uno scompartimento? 11. Che iscrizione portano alcuni scompartimenti? 12. Di che sono carichi i cartelli che s'avvicinano ai treni? 13. Dove mangiano i ricchi quando viaggiano? 14. Dove dormono? 15. Che fa il capostazione? 16. Quale grande stazione d'Italia è stata inaugurata nel 1931?

29. Il treno

Un bello e orribile
mostro si sferra,
corre gli oceani,
corre la terra:

corrusco e fumido
come i vulcani,
i monti supera,
divora i piani;

sorvola i baratri,
poi si nasconde
per antri incogniti,
per vie profonde;

ed esce, e indomito,
di lido in lido,

— Giosuè Carducci

30. Vardiello

Molti e molti anni fa, in un piccolo villaggio non lontano da Napoli, viveva una buona donna, chiamata Grannonia. Ella non aveva che un figlio, Vardiello, ch'era uno scioccone senza pari.

---

18. I pasti in Italia

RECUEIL
DE CHARGES
ET
DE TÊTES
DE DIFFÉRENS CARACTERES;

LEONARD DE VINCI,

Tea Dye

Tea works equally well for staining paper or natural fabrics and comes in handy when you love an item that isn't quite aged enough. My rule of thumb is two tea bags per gallon of water. Simply boil water in a kettle and pour over tea bags laid out in a flat pan. I use an assortment of old enamel pans I've picked up at garage sales, allowing them to stain over the years. For a light stain, let your paper steep for about an hour. For a deeper color, double the amount of tea bags as well as your steeping time. Raspberry tea will lend a pink hue to your items, which is very pretty, but will also smell a bit fruity.

After your items have steeped sufficiently, drain the water and spread them on paper towels to dry overnight. Paper tends to roll up at the edges when dry. It can be flattened under heavy books after it has dried.

You can also try experimenting with coffee. Steep your coffee in a handpress and pour over your paper or fabric. Coffee delivers a deeper, browner tone than tea and also can have an aroma.

Work speaks for itself.

Gifts & Party Favors …

Post Card

For Address only

POSTAGE
DOMESTIC
1 CENT
FOREIGN
2 CENTS

Guest Book

Materials

Composition book, 7" x 9¼"
Old postcard, blank on writing side
Photo corners
Ribbon, 20" piece
Vintage sheet-music booklet
  with appealing cover

Method

•Remove cover from sheet-music booklet
and trim edges with pinking shears. This will
be the new cover for the journal. Adhere new
cover to outside of composition book with
matte medium. Don't forget the back. I also
cover the inside of the covers with the pages
from the music booklet for a nice look. Press all
covers firmly with brayer. Press book overnight
beneath several heavy books.

•Adhere postcard onto front cover with
photo corners and spray adhesive, back side
facing out. Stamp with image. I like to use
old-style French advertising stamps. Title
your book and embellish with other motifs
as you like. This is the time to really personalize your journal, so be creative. I
have been known to use Scrabble pieces
for my initials and rubber stamps that
remind me of far-off lands. Tie ribbon
along spine and embellish with an old-
style key, favorite button, or other item of your
choice. Insert a bookmark for everyday use, such
as pretty business cards from shops, playing
cards, Monopoly money, or others that relate to
the look of the journal.

très petite

La Grande Roue

1/4 INCH ALLOWANCE
MENAGEZ 0.63 CM
DEJESE 0.63 CM

CUT ON THIS LINE
COUPEZ SUR CETTE LIGNE
CORTAR EN ESTE LÍNEA

LA CIUDAD

A CITY

Another Idea . . .

Look for books with graph or staff paper. They make nice gifts for musical or designing friends. For a masculine gift, the graph paper book could be covered with trimmed architectural plans.

Black & White Party Supplies

Materials

Assorted ribbons
Candle jar, 4"
Card stocks,
    black, white, 4" x 6"
Coordinating button
Kraft tag and envelope
Old bingo card

Methods

Invitation: Stamp image on kraft tag. Using double-stick tape, attach tag to white card stock; this will prevent warping. Trim black card stock with scallop-edged scissors. Attach white card stock to trimmed black card stock. Sew a button to the corner if desired. Be aware that hand-canceling will be required at the post office.

Place Tag: Stamp a special quote or tear out a dictionary definition and adhere to tag, using glue stick. Name can be written on reverse side.

Party Favor: Photocopy an image of your choice, mine is the front of an old playing card. Using a glue stick, adhere a strip of schoolbook text around candle jar. Glue image over text, flattening out with clean cloth. Tie ribbon at neck of candle; add a contrasting snippet for detail.

Menu Card: Glue decorative ribbon to bottom of bingo card. (My ribbon came from a soap package.) Use calligraphy or hand-stamp menu with black ink on back of card.

Above: Menu Card

GO

54 75

50 69

48

FREE

42 5

BRADLEY COMPANY
ers of the World's Best Games"
Springfield, Massachusetts

180

when I gr
—I could
They w
and then
mortgage.
"At firs
grim hum
life. Then
good look
"Oh, H
Let me ta
she

MODERN LADY

OU ARE INVITED...

dream (drēm), n. a sequence of
images and thoughts passing
through a sleeping person's mind:
a fanciful vision; a fond hope.

Throw a black and white party
to chase away winter blues. This
ensemble includes a party invitation, menu card, place tag, and
party favor candle jar.

Paper Cones

Materials

Coordinating assorted tassels
Sheet music or decorative paper
Vintage flowers or fill items of choice

Methods

• You may use the pattern for this
project or simply roll the sheet of
paper which will result in a peak at
the back of the cone.

13" cone: Using Pattern for Paper
Cones on page 116, transfer pattern to sheet music and cut out
with pinking shears to 9½" x
12½". Attach tassel with tape
to inside of paper, 3" up from
bottom of longest side on the
right-hand corner.

19" cone: Using Pattern for Paper Cones
on page 116, enlarge 150%. Transfer pattern to
decorative paper and cut with pinking shears to
14½" x 19". Attach tassel with tape to inside of
paper, 6" up from bottom of longest side on the
right-hand corner.

Both cones: Place double-stick tape along inside
edge of paper above the tassel all the way to the
top. Beginning at lower-right corner, curl paper
gently, into a cone shape, capturing the tassel
securely. Gently press taped edge to secure. Fill
cone with vintage flowers or other items.

Place a cone diagonally across each plate at a holiday dinner party. Fill with candy, small trinkets, or a flower bouquet.

REGINA·DI·BASTONE·

symphonie

Milk-glass Jar

Materials

Black ribbon
Rub-on letter sheets
Various-sized milk-glass jars

Method

•Wipe jars clean so they are dust and oil free. Cut out number or letters you would like to use from rub-on letter sheets. Line up letters carefully on jars' surfaces and press firmly and evenly with a burnishing tool such as a wooden craft stick before peeling away. Errors can be "erased" with a razor blade.

•Cut a ribbon length that is double the circumference of each jar and tie a one-sided bow around the necks of the jars.

ABC

W *

3.

* Q

I like to make these as gifts with friend's initials or to number each place setting for an afternoon tea.

33

Musical Fans

Materials

Black acrylic paint
Clothespin, nonpinching type
Ribbon, 24" piece
Sheet music, 10" x 13"
Wooden ice-cream spoon

Method

•Clip clothespin on a piece of cardboard and paint black. Let dry.

•Accordion-fold sheet music lengthwise at ¾" intervals to form a fan.

•Tuck base of fan all the way into clothespin opening. Insert ice-cream spoon into center of clothespin at back of fan to create a spine. Tuck a small flower into front of fan.

•Lay fan flat at center of ribbon and wind ribbon around clothespin, right over left and back again until you reach the clothespin base. Knot in front and trim if desired.

Flutes off

LE COUSIN PONS

277

LE COUSIN PONS

...sin Pons, écrit en juin 1846, forme avec La Cousine
...t il est inséparable, une sorte de diptyque : Les
...pauvres. Balzac a expliqué l'idée commune des deux
...s une lettre à Mme Hanska : « Le Vieux Musicien,
...rimitif du Cousin Pons, — est le parent pauvre,
...humiliations, d'injures, plein de cœur, pardonnant
...se vengeant que par des bienfaits. La Cousine Bette
...accablée d'humiliations, d'injures, vivant
...familles, et y méditant
...et de ses

...aussi Le Vieux M...

...n compositeur de musique, ancien prix de
...heure de célébrité, mais qui, vieilli et
...t en donnant des leçons de piano. De son
...apporté l'amour des objets d'art, et sa
...eur, servie par un goût délicat et un
...s de réunir chez lui, à peu de frais, un
...sin Pons, célibataire besogneux et gour-
...an au XIXe siècle.

10

Strings off

I was awed one afternoon by a beautiful old music book with a green velvet cover. It had water damage, but I knew many of the pages could still be used for something. You can use these fanciful fans as favors at a piano recital or a pre-concert gathering.

Gift Adornments

Materials

Assorted buttons
Assorted dimensional embellishments
Assorted index cards
Old sepia-toned photographs
Ribbon
Rickrack

Method

•Color-copy the old photographs and trim with decorative-edged scissors. Enlarge or reduce your photocopies to better fit your cards.

•Be inventive when adhering the image to the card. For variety, capture some within photo corners. Attach others with a small clothespin or paper clip, in addition to the glue stick. Press flat with brayer.

•For dimensional embellishments attach rickrack, a bingo game piece, or an old typewriter key with craft glue or simply stitch a special button on tag. Don't be shy with your adornments. View your tags as little art pieces.

•Punch a hole, then pull ribbon through and knot. Be generous. Double up the ribbon for more impact. You can write the recipient's name on the back with a calligraphy pen.

Embellish your gifts with over-sized tags and present the recipient with two gifts in one.

Party Favor Cones

Materials

Assorted fabric trims and laces
Assorted fill items
Black acrylic paint
Broad felt-tip pen, gold
Cardboard yarn cones, 7"
Ribbon, 20" piece
Sheet music

Method

•Adhere sheet music to cone with matte medium, overlapping with smaller torn pieces as needed. Allow paper to fold over top to inside of cone as necessary.

•Paint inside of cone black, covering folded in paper, up sides to top rim. Edge top of cone with a broad felt-tip gold pen.

•Drill ⅛" holes on two opposite sides, ¼" down from top edge.

•Choose fabric trim as desired, measure and cut before adhering with craft glue. Glue trim just underneath the drilled holes. I chose purple pom-poms with an antique lace detail layered on top. One wayward pom-pom was then adhered to the bottom of the cone with craft glue. You could also use a colorful tassel. Embellish with buttons along edge of trim if desired.

•Thread ribbon from inside cone to out, using a large-eyed embroidery needle. Leave 6" on either side to tie a knot or a bow, looping back over the ribbon left for hanging. Fill with shredded paper and special whatnots for guests.

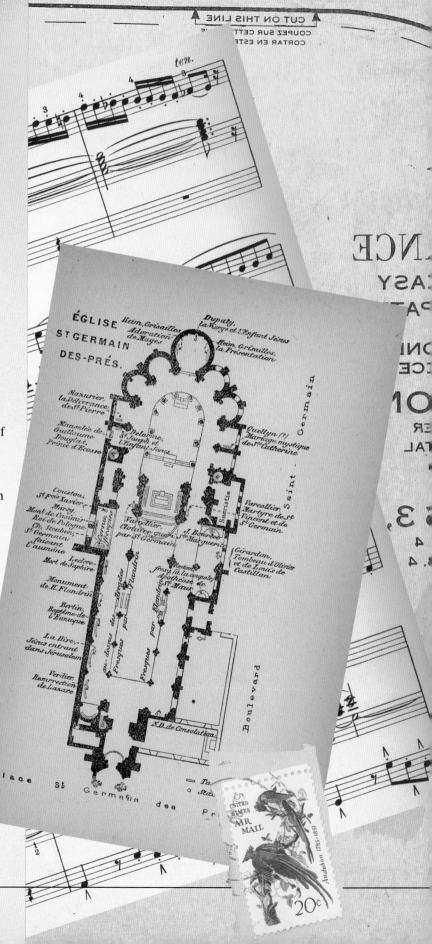

Hang these at your mantel for each guest to choose as a party favor.

Work speaks
for itself.

-USE-

Lautz Bros. & Co's

PURE AND HEALTHY

SOAPS.

Try them! They are the Best Soaps in the Market.

Tea-dyed Tags

Materials

Black tea
Manila tags, 2¼" x 4½"
Ribbon
Vintage wrapping paper

Method

•Dye tags according to Tea Dye
instructions on page 21 and allow to
dry overnight.

•Cut out images from wrapping paper
with deckle-edged scissors. Glue to tag.
You can also use rubber stamps as the
image itself. Embellish with polka dots, a
checkered pattern, postmarks, and words.
Stamp "to" and "from" on back. Tie groups
of six together with a ribbon.

After many requests for the tags I used on gifts over the years, I decided to offer tag sets as the gift itself.

1/4 INCH ALLOWANCE
MÉNAGEZ 0.63 CM
DEIXE 0.63 CM

CUT ON THIS LINE
COUPEZ SUR CETTE LIGNE
CORTAR EN ESTE LÍNEA

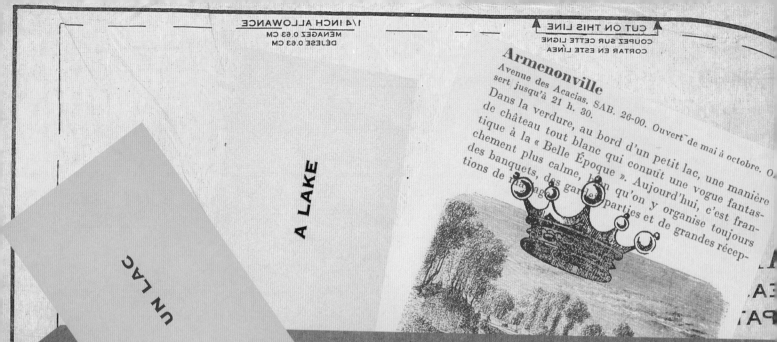

A LAKE

UN LAC

Armenonville
Avenue des Acacias. SAB. 26-00. Ouvert de mai à octobre. O...
sert jusqu'à 21 h. 30.
Dans la verdure, au bord d'un petit lac, une manière
de château tout blanc qui connut une vogue fantas-
tique à la « Belle Époque ». Aujourd'hui, c'est fran-
chement plus calme, bien qu'on y organise toujours
des banquets, des gar... parties et de grandes récep-
tions de ma...

Another Idea . . .

These tags can be
used in many ways. To use
them as name tags, simply
insert a safety pin. For
bookmarks, leave one side
blank; or for luggage tags,
stamp address on back.
You may want to laminate
the luggage tag to protect
it during your trips.

A l'Ange Gardien
E. LAILLET — CHARTRES

Decorative Candles

Materials

Assorted ribbons
Candle jars, 4", 8"
  with white unscented candles
Old book, 4" x 6"
Vintage trading cards

Methods

Large candle:

•Tear small book pages in half and adhere horizontally to candle jar, 2" from top lip. Color-copy a favorite trading card and trim with decorative-edged scissors. Adhere slightly off-center over book page on candle. Press firmly with a clean, dry cloth to smooth out all wrinkles.

•Tie a one-sided bow around candle rim. Loop additional 3" piece of ribbon around knot of bow to garnish. Be certain to trim wick to ½" and do not leave unattended while burning.

Small candle:

•Tear small book page into quarters and stamp image in center. I stamp right over text. Center and glue to front of candle. Tie ribbon at top.

My friend introduced me to the idea of adorning candle jars. These are my versions, which work equally well for collecting or burning.

ADMIT ONE
8993127

MERCI

84 93
ADMIT ONE
844093

SAINTE-BEUVE
(1804-1869)

Vintage Hangers

Materials

Assorted embellishments
Ribbon, 10" piece
Vintage hangers

Method

•If my hangers aren't already imprinted, I will rubber-stamp a whimsical saying: ooh la la, violà, ma chemise, c'est bon, or a person's name.

•Tie a generous, one-sided bow with ribbon at the center of the hanger. Wire-edged ribbon holds its shape nicely, but floppy bows can be equally charming. Add embellishments such as more ribbon or buttons tied on with string. I've also used big wooden alphabet beads, velvet flowers, little plastic fruits, even silver jacks tied on with wire. A decorative hang tag makes a nice final touch.

A basket of wooden hangers tumbled out at my feet during our town's sidewalk sale. I scooped up an armful and made sets for special friends.

Handmade Cards

Materials

Blank card, 5" x 7",
    with matching envelope
Dictionary illustrations
Glassine envelopes, 3½" x 2¼"
Postage stamps
Rayon ribbon, 14" piece
Sheet music

Method

• Trim music scraps to tuck inside glassine envelopes. Adhere small illustration or postage stamp on music scrap before inserting scrap into glassine envelope. I often also sprinkle in a bit of lavender or poppy seeds. Pumpkin seeds or crushed leaves and rose petals also look nice. Seal envelope with glue stick.

• Attach a strip of double-stick tape to top and bottom of glassine envelope length-wise and press flat to card.

• Tie a one-sided bow at top. Add an extra sprig of ribbon, lace or button as an accent.

Tip: Rubber-stamp a small image on the inside of your card and on the envelope as a nice surprise.

Handmade cards are simply
better to receive.

FOR YOU

FOR YOU

Whiling Away an Afternoon . . .

Collage Bottles

Materials

Assorted old bottles
Decorative papers
Denture-cleaning tablet
Old books

Ribbon
Various vintage postage stamps

Method

•Clean the bottles by soaking them in hot
water and a denture-cleaning tablet. This
takes away the grimiest dirt but doesn't
clean so thoroughly that all sense of age
is gone. I like the glass to be a bit
cloudy.

•Tear portions of the book's pages
to cover the face of the bottle and
overlap the edges. Apply the torn
pages to the bottles with matte
medium, pressing out all creases
with a clean cloth. Add a
postage stamp and scallop-
edged decorative paper. I
paint my own striped paper
and add a rubber-stamped
postmark for additional
interest. To make Striped
Paper refer to page 20. Tie a
simple ribbon bow around the neck
of the bottle.

Brookside Park, Dover, Pa.

These bottles look beautiful lined up on a bathroom ledge or kitchen windowsill. Place a single flower stem in one and leave the others empty.

Little Art Piece

Materials

⅛"-thick plywood, 5" x 10"
22-gauge copper wire, 20" piece
Coordinating acrylic paint
Fabric trim, 6" piece
Ribbon
Vintage postcard
Vintage wallpaper scraps
Wallpaper or decorative paper

Method

•Paint sides and back of plywood with
acrylic paint. Adhere wallpaper or decorative paper to plywood with spray mount
and roll flat with brayer.

•Trim the postcard with decorative-
edged scissors. Attach the postcard to
the plywood with spray mount. You may want to
color copy the postcard onto card stock if the
original is too thick or has personal value.
Define borders of postcard with decorative ribbon and a trimmed wallpaper scrap. Adhere with
craft glue and roll flat. Glue fabric trim to bottom of plywood, allowing both ends to wrap
around to the back of the plywood to prevent
fraying.

•Drill two 1/16" holes, ½" down from top of plywood. Thread copper wire through holes to create a hanger. Allow wire to twist and turn to add
character to the overall look.

This piece is the result of a love affair with materials. How could I pass up that beautiful hand-tinted postcard or sweet l'amour toujours ribbon? The tasseled trim was simply the icing on the cake!

BONNE ANNÉE

l'amour toujours

Cache Pot, Canisters & Sewing Kit

Materials

French advertising labels, postcards,
 book illustrations
Old book
Ribbon
Various-shaped weathered tins

Method

•Color-copy the images to fit your container. Mine were found on the back side of vintage trading cards. The Eiffel Tower was a lucky find at a postcard sale, and the bird came from an old English woodcut illustration book.

•Adhere images with matte medium and press flat with clean cloth. For larger surfaces, you may want to add a text background as I did by cutting a circle to fit the sewing kit's lid.

•Measure a ribbon length double the lid's circumference and tie a generous bow around lid.

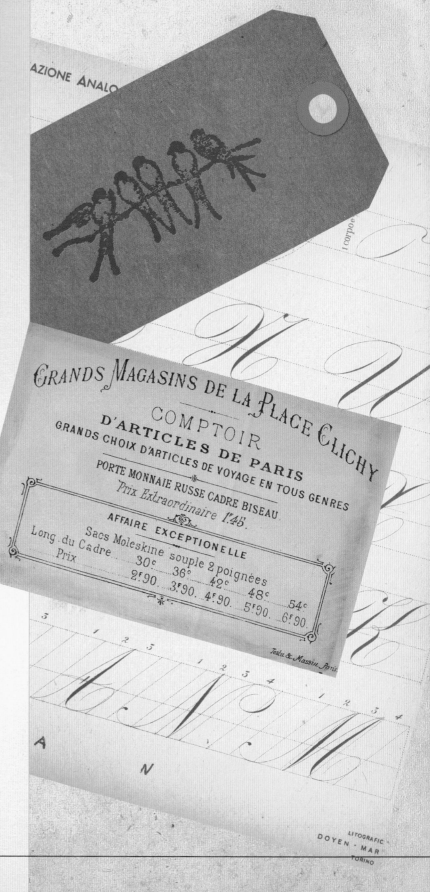

cache
pot

EPICERIES, VINS & COMESTIBLES

FONTAINE

172, Faubourg Saint-Antoine, 172

PARIS

La Maison se recommande
ses cafés et appelle l'
non café à **2 fr.** 1

Eau
de
Toilette
CH. FAY
9, Rue de la Paix
PARIS

A neighbor passed these fabulous tins over her fence one day and a friend dropped by with her grandmother's sewing kit. Both offerings were great fun to enhance. Store tea bags in your canisters and colorful wooden thread spools in the sewing kit.

Collage with Beeswax

Materials

⅛"-thick plywood, 5" x 7½"
22-gauge steel wire
Assorted papers with text, colors, and images
Beeswax
Black acrylic paint
Ribbon

Method

• Paint back and sides of plywood black.

• Arrange your collage. I usually begin with a larger background piece and have a central image in mind. I rearrange smaller pieces until I have a composition I like. This takes some time and you need to be patient.

• Adhere collage to plywood one piece at a time with matte medium. You may want to make small pencil marks to indicate position of certain pieces. Roll flat with brayer.

• Refer to Beeswax on pages 18–19 for instructions to coat the collage with wax. Avoid hanging your collage in direct sunlight.

• Drill ¹⁄₁₆" hole, ¼" down at both sides of top. Push wire through, leaving 1½" on each end to twist around the hanging loop. Tie ribbon on one side as an accent.

Tip: When making your collage, vary the edges of the elements, keep some straight and tear others. Try placing items sideways or upside down. Carry a certain color from one corner to another. Place a photograph corner or postage stamp to link two unresolved areas.

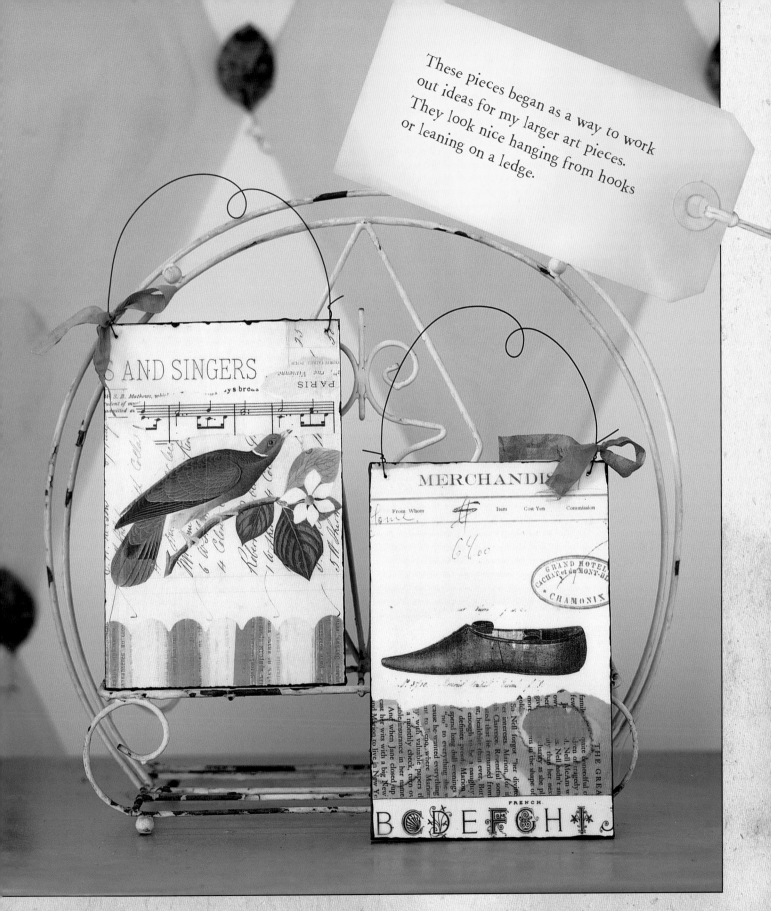

These pieces began as a way to work out ideas for my larger art pieces. They look nice hanging from hooks or leaning on a ledge.

31

A FLOWER

très petite

Another Idea . . .

As you work on various projects, think about setting aside special fragments or embellishments for use in more serious or involved pieces. Consider themes you may want to explore.

LATEST STYLES

BEST MATERIAL.

REYNOLDS BROTHERS,

CELEBRATED FOR FINE SHOES

LADIES, MISSES & CHILDREN.
ARE MANUFACTURED AT UTICA, N.Y.

These Goods are acknowledged by all to be THE BEST MADE and may be found on sale in the principal Cities and Towns of the United States.

SUPERIOR FINISH

PERFECT FITTING.

margin   of   error

Picket Fence Icon

Materials

28-gauge steel wire
Acrylic paint
Alphabet beads
Picket fence top, 2½" x 8¼"
Ribbon, 10"
Small copper nails
Tarot card
Various found objects

Method

•Drill a ⅛" hole, ½" down from peak of fence top. Paint picket with two coats of acrylic. My first icons were from beautifully weathered white wood, so I left them as is.

•Adhere tarot card with spray mount. Roll with a brayer for best adhesion. Embellish with objects that you have collected, such as vintage buttons, charms, or glass beads. If objects have holes, I like to attach them with nails or pins. All others can be glued.

•Choose a word to reflect the mood you feel from the card you have chosen. String alphabet beads on wire and wrap around nail heads on either side. Pull ribbon through hole with large-eyed needle, knot, and hang.

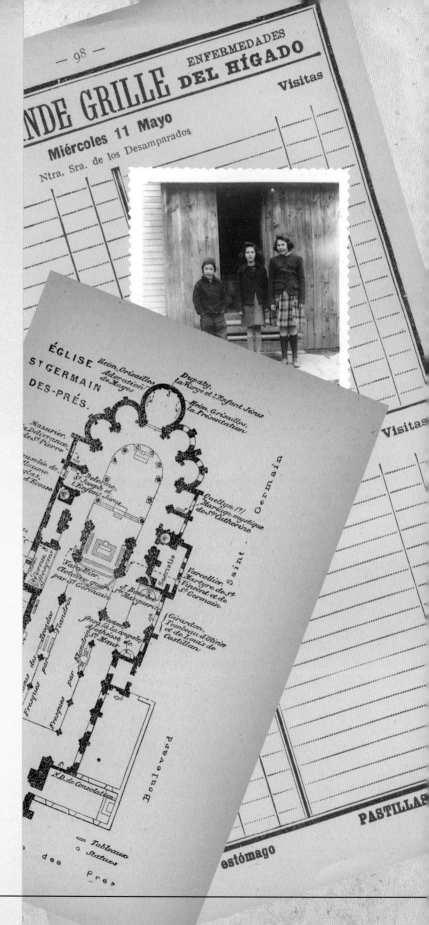

A section of picket fence that had been taken down at our farmhouse sat against the barn for months before I finally convinced my husband to saw off the picket tops for my latest idea.

DREAM

XVII

LE STELLE

23 24

Figment

Materials

⅛"-thick plywood, 7" x 8"
Buttons
Decorative paper
Old book
Photo corners
Postcard
Round-headed fasteners
Screw eye
Silk ribbon, 20" piece
Tassel
Velvet ribbon, 7" piece

Method

•Tear out two pages from old book and cut to fit front and back of plywood. I used pages from a vintage French dictionary. Adhere with matte medium, pressing firmly with your brayer. Tape all edges, allowing tape to extend ⅛" onto front and back.

•Cut decorative paper to 7" x 4". Use pinking shears at bottom edge, which will extend slightly past plywood. I used a beautiful hand-stitched sample. Adhere with matte medium. Glue velvet ribbon at intersection of the two papers with craft glue.

•Color copy postcard onto card stock if desired and cut out with pinking shears. Place image into photo corners and, using spray mount, set into place 1" from top. Press as firmly as possible. Image will be raised slightly as it passes over the velvet ribbon.

•Drill ⅛" holes, ½" down from top of plywood. Capture your silk ribbon by placing the round-headed fasteners through the plywood. I added gold cord as an accent around the fasteners, before completely securing. Twist small screw eye into center bottom of plywood. Attach tassel with thread or thin copper wire. Use craft glue to adhere buttons to the velvet. Floral leaves in a contrasting color look pretty as well.

I call this piece a figment to remind us
of the possibilities of our imagination.

Framed Fable

Materials

Black acrylic paint
Dried flower
Hang tag
Leaf skeleton
Old map
Ribbons, 20" pieces (2)
Thumbtacks
Unfinished frame, 5" x 7"
Vintage postcard and photograph

Method

•Paint frame black and sand lightly.

•Arrange collage on face of postcard. Use photographs and mementos with a particular "story" in mind. Try to limit yourself to just a few items as this simplicity will provide the most impact in such a small frame.

•I adhered my photograph with double-stick tape and photo corners to prevent warping. Enjoying the delicate transparency of the leaf skeleton, I dabbed the stem with white glue and carefully laid it in place. The same was done with the dried flower. Both harken back to some long ago day in the photographed women's lives.

•Place collage against glass in frame and insert cardboard to secure. To cover back of frame, I used an old map trimmed to fit with pinking shears and secured with double-stick tape.

•Cut hang tag to 1" wide. Type or stamp a saying onto white paper. Mine is a snippet of poetry. Trim and adhere to tag with glue stick.

•Attach the hanging ribbon to the top corners of the frame back by piercing the ribbon with a thumbtack. Tie decorative ribbon around base of frame and tie your tag with thread or thin wire to the bow.

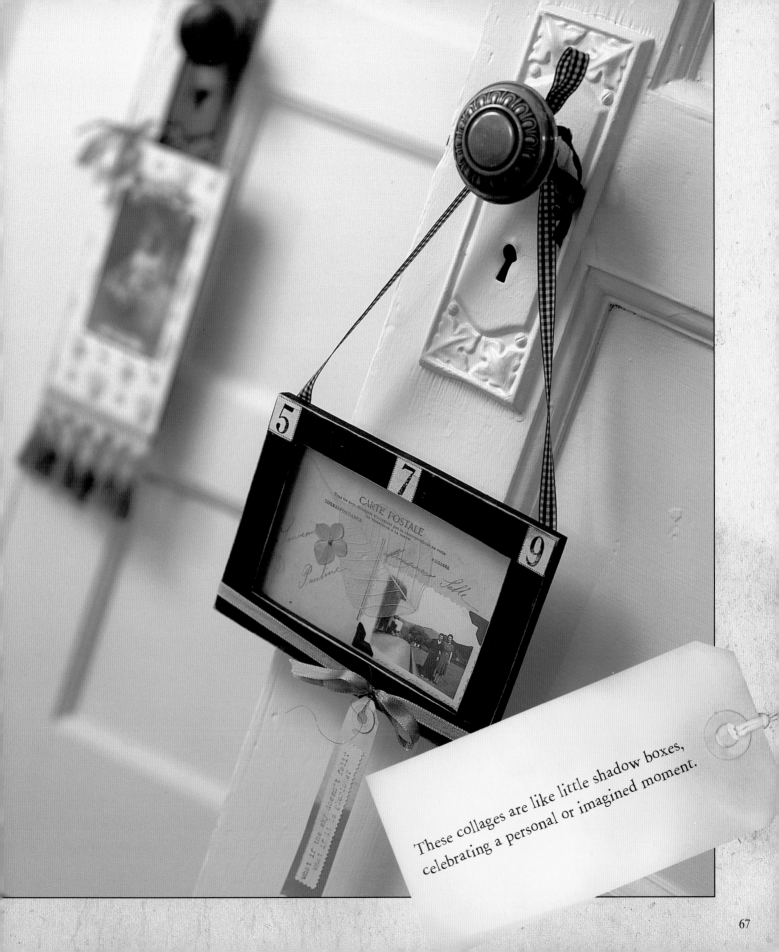

CARTE POSTALE

These collages are like little shadow boxes, celebrating a personal or imagined moment.

Home Away From Home

Materials

Corrugated cardboard, 11" x 5½"
Old map
Twine, 12' piece
Wooden bead (2)
Wooden clothespins with spring (16)

Method

•Trim old map to fit cardboard and adhere with matte medium. Press flat with brayer.

•Stamp top of each clothespin with one letter to spell "Home Away From Home." Clamp clothespins to top of cardboard.

•Wrap twine around board, tying at front with a simple bow. Thread a wooden bead onto each end of twine tails and knot in place.

This tucks easily in a suitcase for drying small items when traveling.

Stacking Boxes

Materials

Acrylic paint
Assorted striped papers
Plain cardboard boxes: 7" square,
   6" circle, and 3" x 4" rectangle
Rayon seam-binding ribbon
Vintage trading cards

Method

•Paint each box lid to complement the trading card image you have chosen. Allow to dry.

•Trim striped paper to height of box bottom and apply with matte medium, overlapping a page as needed as you go around the box.

•Adhere your trading card, or a color copy of card, to the center of the lid. If there is room, you can affix a trimmed textbook page first to serve as a border for your card. Press out wrinkles with a clean cloth.

•Cut a ribbon length the circumference of the box plus 10" and tie around lid. Ribbon will stay secure if your bow is firmly tied.

•I like to stamp an image on the bottom of the inside of the box for a little surprise.

I think the more the merrier when it comes to boxes. Keep a collection for whatever comes along—old toys, gift tags, jewelry, or seashells.

Special Indulgences . . .

Jewelry Holder

Materials

16-gauge soft copper wire
20-gauge copper or brass sheet, 3" x 8"
Acrylic paint
Copper nails
Pine board, 6" x 10" x ½"
Steel or copper rod, 16" piece
Weathered finial

Method

•Use Pattern for Jewelry Holder on page 117 or draw around your own hand on the pine board. Make certain the grain runs vertically with the fingers. With a scroll saw (fast) or a jigsaw (slow), cut out hand.

•Paint the hand with colors of your choice. I used a combination of parchment, white, and Naples yellow, sanding between layers and rubbing in highlights with my thumb. Allow to dry.

•Drill ⅛" hole, 1½" up from center bottom of hand. Do the same in the center of the finial to 2" deep. Be very careful about drilling straight.

•Cut a 6" piece of rod, insert into finial and set with light tap of a hammer. Using a small vice and pliers, create a wavy pattern in another 6" piece of rod. Don't worry about perfection. Attach rods together, using wire and a crisscross loop pattern.

•Cut out heart from copper or brass sheet with tin snips according to Pattern for Jewelry Holder. Drill three ¹⁄₁₆" holes at each point of the heart. Nail heart in place on the hand. With a gentle twisting motion, attach hand to metal rod. If the hand wobbles, a small amount of epoxy putty or carpenter's glue will solve the problem.

WRITE

When a Neiman-Marcus opened in our town a few years back, my husband and I went to ogle the store displays and beautiful merchandise. What we came home with, however, was not jewelry or designer clothes but rather a half dozen chipped up, old finials, imported from India. They sat in my studio for almost a year before I had an idea for them.

Floral Shoe Form

Materials

Assorted velvet flowers
Tag
Various ribbons
Vintage shoe form

Method

•Stamp a saying letter-by-letter around the edge of the toe. Be imaginative with your quote. Think about steps and journeys.

•Tie a one-sided bow through arch of shoe, using a 20" length of ribbon. Create a small arrangement with the velvet leaves and flowers. Wrap the wire stems of the arrangement firmly around bow's knot to accent. Attach a tag to the stem of the arrangement to personalize the project.

STEP LIGHTLY

STEP LIGHTLY

STEP LIGHTLY

anna corba • found cat

I found these shoe forms piled high at an antique fair. I've also seen them in various vintage shops. They look pretty on a bookshelf and also come in handy as paperweights.

Candy Dish

Materials

Assorted fabric trims
Black acrylic paint
Old book
Various-shaped martini glasses

Method

•Adhere book pages, some intact and some ripped, to outside of glass with matte medium. Begin at top of stem and allow edges to overlap top of glass. Pay attention to the look of the pages both inside and outside of the glass. A well-placed illustration or chapter title creates interest to either view. Allow to dry thoroughly. Trim around top with very sharp scissors, using the glass edge as your guide.

•Paint glass base with two coats of black acrylic, including the underside of the base. After drying thoroughly, apply one coat of matte medium to seal. This also gives a crackled effect to the paint.

•Cut fabric trim and attach neatly at top edge with craft glue. Tie contrasting ribbon in a bow around glass stem.

I fill these with peanuts and choco-
late kisses for parties. Arranged in a
group, these dishes are striking for
any special occasion.

Paper Doll

Materials

22-gauge wire
Buttons: one large, three small
Fabric trim
Fiberboard, 20" x 18"
Old book
One-gallon container
Ribbon
Wire dress form, 13"

Method

•Fill container with water until two-thirds full. Tear out 6–10 sheets from book. I like to use a theme such as birds, botanical, French text, or whatever inspires me. Crumple all pages into loose balls and immerse one at a time into water. Smooth out each sheet carefully on fiberboard and brush with matte medium. Carefully lay over wire form at an artful angle. Continue with more pages until entire form is covered, overlapping as needed and tucking bottom edges to the inside. Sit form on waxed paper to let dry overnight.

•Attach a large button at breast with wire. Tie ribbon around the neck and glue fabric trim around waist. Add flowers or leaves as desired. Sometimes I wrap a beautiful scrap of lace around the waist as well, tying a knot in the back. Tie bows at artful intervals by threading a wide needle in and out of wire form. Embellish by gluing a trio of buttons at spots where your papers overlap.

These dolls look adorable in a little girl's room, tied up with her favorite colors.

Decorative Tray

Materials

Acrylic paints: black, cinnamon-
    apple red, leaf green,
Acrylic varnish
Color postcard
Old book
Wallpaper or decorative paper
Wire-edged ribbon, black-and-white checkered
Wooden tray, 14" x 11"

Method

•Paint entire tray cinnamon-apple red. Let dry.
Accent along edges and joints with leaf green.
Apply another coat of red. When dry, sand
back to allow green to peek through in spots.

•Glue whole pages torn from an old book
onto tray face using matte medium, overlapping as necessary to fill entire space. I used
a French dictionary. Enlarge your color
postcard on the copier to 11" x 7". Trim
with deckle-edged scissors and glue to
book-page background.

•Cut wallpaper or decorative paper with scallop-
edged scissors to fit length of tray; glue to top
and bottom borders. Add miscellaneous collage
elements as desired. Keep the composition simple, as the postcard is the main point. I included
a circular French bistro card and a stamped
manila tag.

•Apply black polka dots around edges of tray
with a blunt round paintbrush. I simply eyeball
the distance between dots, allowing for a handmade quality. Varnish top, sides, and bottom of
tray twice, allowing to dry thoroughly between
coats. Tie black-and-white checkered ribbon to
handles for a final decorative touch.

BIARRITZ. - La Mairie

A TRAY FOR THINGS

I found these wonderful oversized postcard reproductions in a dusty shop in France and felt they could be worth inventing a project around, and voilà!

LE MÉDECIN DE CAMPAGNE   275

autres qui ne sont pas commodes du tout, le tenaient
si bien pour autre chose qu'un homme, qu'ils respectaient son pavillon en disant qu'y toucher c'était se
frotter à Dieu. Il régnait sur le monde entier, tandis que 110
...rte de la France. Alors
...ille de noix d'Égypte,
...angla...

HENRY ROWLANDS,
JEWELER & SILVERSMITH,
Importer of
DIAMONDS,
WATCHES, CLOCKS,
Opera Glasses and Fancy Goods.

A Large Display of
Silver and Plated Ware.

NEW GOODS RECEIVED DAILY.

7 North
CORNER MAIDE
BANY

Cake Pedestals

Materials

½"-thick plywood
3M Scotch Glue Tape
Acrylic paints: black, ivory
Acrylic varnish
Card stock
Fabric trim, 32"
Fence post finial or
    old spindle
Flat-headed wood screw
Glue gun/glue sticks
Golden oak furniture wax
Vintage sheet-music booklet
    with appealing cover

Method

•Choose 8"–9" tall finial or
spindle and cut flat at top. Base
must be wide enough so that pedestal doesn't
tip. Cut out 10" circle from plywood. Drill ⅛"
hole in center.

•Attach circle to finial with countersunk flat-
headed screw (a little wood glue doesn't hurt).
Fill depression with wood filler and sand entire
top smooth when dry.

•Paint finial base with one coat ivory acrylic.
Paint over the ivory with two coats black acrylic,
allowing paint to dry thoroughly between coats.
Sand slightly at edges to allow ivory to peek
through at spots. Wax and buff base according to
directions on wax can.

•Cut vintage music cover to fit the 10" circle top.
Adhere with matte medium, being certain to
smooth out all air bubbles with a clean cloth.
Start at center and press out toward sides. Let
dry overnight. Apply two coats of varnish, one
horizontally, one vertically, allowing to dry in
between.

•Cut card stock to 1⅛" width, using scallop-
edged scissors. All colors can look nice, depend-
ing on your music cover. Wrap glue tape around
edge of circle, press firmly and peel back covering of tape. Press card stock firmly in place
against glue tape.

•Overlay fabric trim at top edge of card stock,
using a glue gun. I glue about 3" at a time, using
the glue sparingly so as not to get drips. Be
patient and trim neatly at the seam, pressing
ends of trim together to meet.

•On smaller pedestals, you can leave off the card
stock and simply use pom-pom trim. This is a
cute look for pedestals used for decoration only.

I make my pedestals in four sizes: 12" for cakes, 10" for tortes, 8" for a cup-cake or two, and 6" as a sweet jewelry stand for a dresser.

½ INCH ALLOWANCE
MÉNAGEZ 0.63 CM
DEJESE 0.63 CM

CUT ON THIS LINE
COUPEZ SUR CETTE LIGNE
CORTAR EN ESTE LÍNEA

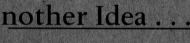

Another Idea . . .

Use these pedestals in and out of the dining room. A stack of three pedestals make a special centerpiece. Outside of the dining room, display guest towels on the largest and showcase jewelry on the smallest.

Sleepy Hanger

Materials

⅛"-thick plywood, 10½" x 7"
22-gauge wire, 24" piece (2)
Decorative tassel
Masking tape
Old book
Ribbon
Striped paper
Wooden hanger

Method

•Using matte medium, cover front and back of plywood with book pages. Blank ledger pages or yellowed graph paper works well, so as not to compete with your text. Roll flat with brayer. Tape around all edges of plywood with masking tape. An edge of about ⅛" should be visible on both sides.

•Stamp your quote. I used a sleepy quote as I hung this on my bedroom door. You could use a favorite nursery rhyme to place over a child's bed. Don't be too concerned with lining up your letters perfectly, slight imperfections add to the charm.

•Drill ⅛" holes at top of plywood, ½" in from sides. Also drill holes 2" up arms of hanger on both sides. Insert wire at board to shape a large V. Twist once and bring one end through hanger to meet other end of V shape. Twist several times. I added a little velvet flower to disguise the final twist. Tie decorative tassel at hanger's center. Add more ribbons as desired.

•Cut 10½" strip of striped paper into an elongated zigzag pattern. Refer to Striped Paper on page 20. Place double-sided tape along top at edge and press in place onto plywood. Zigzags will extend below board.

And their tales to relate;
So shed at the door your daily scheme
And enter the twilight
Of the waking dream

279

sleep hath its own
world... and dreams...
have breath
and tears
and tortures
and the touch of joy.

LORD BYRON

Michael Tschantz-Han
Oppenheimer
Abet

QUIET

13 14 15 16 17 18 19

ITURE CO.,   Clay, 13

I hoard quotes like candy. These
pieces are a way to display some
of my favorites.

Five Birds Bowl

Materials

Acrylic paints: black, gold
Bird rubber stamp
Pages from dictionary
Used wooden bowl

Method

•Stamp five birds on various dictionary pages; use bird-related definitions if desired. Allow ink to dry.

•Tear some pages while leaving others whole. Have about 15 pieces to choose from. Applying matte medium to each page at a time, attach to inside of bowl, composing as you go along. Press the pages firmly into the curve of the bowl with your brush, allowing some matte medium to help seal pages. Allow page edges to extend above rim of bowl by at least ½". After drying thoroughly, trim page tops, using edge of bowl as your guide.

•Paint entire outside of bowl black. After drying, apply gold stripes around edge with ¼" brush. Sand lightly.

My husband fills this bowl with bread crusts and feeds the birds outside his vegetable garden.

Creating Memories . . .

Keepsake Envelopes

Materials

Photocopied images
Ribbon
Tickets
Various-colored envelopes, 11" x 9"

Method

•Trim photocopied images with decorative-edged scissors. I used a Spanish tarot deck that I found in Madrid. Use glue stick to adhere image onto envelope, pressing firmly. Embellish further with rubber stamps. I keep my envelopes "anonymous" looking. You may want to consider a particular theme such as an opera cover for a special-occasion envelope or a uniquely addressed postcard for a correspondence envelope.

•Punch two holes horizontally, 1" from bottom of envelope flap. Bring both ends of ribbon up from underneath and tie into soft bow. Flap will not actually attach to envelope. Punch a hole in one end of a movie or amusement-park ticket and string onto bow on envelope flap.

Use these oversized envelopes to collect special cards and correspondence. I have one for favorite photographs, one for mementos from special events, and one for unique scraps used in my collages.

Keepsake Box

Materials

Acrylic paints: black, gold, deep green
Assorted fabric trims
Cigar box, 7" square
Sepia-toned postcard

Method

•Paint the entire surface of box deep green. Paint the inside of box black. Paint lightly over all green surfaces with gold. Rub through the gold paint with your thumb while paint is still damp. Lightly sand when dry. Add a wash of black to bottom of box to deepen the green tone. Lightly sand when dry. I often go back and forth with this process a few times to achieve a richly layered effect.

•Adhere postcard to box top with spray mount and press flat with brayer. The postcard can be color copied onto card stock if it is precious or you can use an old family photograph. Define top and bottom borders of postcard by gluing on fabric trim with craft glue. I wrapped the bottom border around the sides of the lid for a more interesting composition. Tie a glass bead or velvet leaves with wire around box clasp.

I was given stacks of empty cigar boxes for storage by a friend of my father. I figured they would look much prettier when decorated.

Garden Thoughts Book

Materials

Botanical print
Old binder pages, 8½" x 11"
Paper with holes punched to match
   binder pages
Silk ribbon, 36" piece
Water-based paints

Method

•Personalize the botanical print by lightly
washing with thinned down acrylic or water-
color paints. Allow to dry thoroughly before
gluing to the binder page that will be the
front cover. Roll flat with brayer. Rubber-
stamp your title, such as "in the garden" or
"gathering notes." Play with the garden theme.

•Assemble the front cover binder page, paper,
and a plain binder page together to create a
book. Thread ribbon from front through top and
bottom holes of the binder pages. Bring both
ends out through middle hole and tie a bow. Tie
loosely so that book can expand as things are
added to it.

This makes a great informal
scrapbook for garden musings.

Fler. Jap. p. 29 & Tab. 31.

JOURNEYS
IN
MY
OWN
BACKYARD

HYPERICUM japonicum.

Pastime Books

Materials

Brown paper lunch bags (6)
Clothespin
Colored pencil
Silk ribbon, 25" piece
Vintage seed packets or image relating
   to your theme

Method

•Stack paper bags, alternating open and
closed ends on the right side. Fold in half
one at a time and punch holes at top and
bottom, ¾" from edge and ½" from spine.
Place folded bags, one inside the other to
create assembled book.

•Trim front of seed packet with decorative-
edged scissors and adhere to front cover with
glue stick. Press this bag flat with brayer and
refold. With all bags back together, thread
ribbon through holes from behind and tie a
generous bow at front.

•Add embellishments as desired at bow, such as
glass or wooden letter beads, a child's fork, or
simply more ribbon. Use clothespin to capture
pencil alongside book for easy note taking.

•Pages that are the open side of the bags can be
used for storing treasures.

OUR NEST

REGNO D'ITALIA

LET'S EAT

TURNIP
SEVEN TOP
CARD SEED CO
60

BEET
EARLY BLOOD TURNIP
CARD SEED CO
B₃

GARDEN NOTES

I love these little books for jotting notes and collecting seeds while walking in the garden. I recently moved and made a series to collect ideas and material samples while shopping for my new home.

Recipe Book

Materials

Blank journal, spiral or cloth-bound,
   8½" x 11"
Manila tags
Various paper scraps, including recipes

Method

• Cover front of journal by adhering large ledger page or other paper cut to fit, with matte medium. Press flat with brayer. Repeat for back cover.

• Create collage with various torn recipes and other food-type ephemera. I included stained tea bags and food flash cards. Adhere with glue stick and roll flat. Embellish with stamped images and dimensional objects. I used bingo pieces because I liked the red accent.

• Decide how many chapters you would like and stamp a hang tag with each heading. Place sideways into book and attach with glue stick and photograph corners.

• I included a craft envelope in the inside cover of my book to hold recipes waiting to be tried. Don't forget a luscious bookmark; rubber-stamp an oversized hang tag and string with rickrack.

I consider one's recipe book to be as personal as a diary. This one has plenty of room for clippings and dinner party anecdotes.

Photograph Collage

Materials

⅛"-thick plywood, 5½" x 7"
28-gauge steel wire, 15" piece
Black acrylic paint
Black-and-white family photographs
Old book
Ribbon snippet

Method

•Paint back and edges of
plywood black.

•Using matte medium,
cover front with page torn
from book and trim to fit. I try to find a
chapter heading that will make a fun caption.

•Color-copy your photograph. Enlarge or reduce
as necessary to fit. Trim with decorative-edged
scissors. Apply with matte medium over book
page. Press flat with brayer.

•Add other snippets of text or border to create
interest. I found mine by perusing through a
grammar book with interesting graphic details.
Apply beeswax for a muted, aged look, according to Beeswax instructions on pages 18–19.

•Drill ⅟₁₆" hole, ¼" down at both sides of top.
Push wire through, leaving 1½" on each end to
twist around the hanging loop. Tie ribbon to one
side as accent.

Tip: Try making these in a
smaller size, 3½" x 2½", and
insert into a cellophane bag
with a stamped saying to
match the photograph ("go
baby", "friends for life", "hugs
and kisses"). I call these "fortune cookies" and they make
great little party favors.

At your next family reunion make
a collage for each family member,
using a photograph long forgotten
but not lost.

Travel Bags

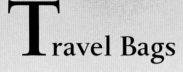

Materials

Brown paper lunch bags (14)
Clothespins, nonpinching type (2)
Vintage postcard
Wire-edged ribbon, 21" piece

Method

•Stack bags one on top of the other. Face front-cover bag so that its opening is to the right. Face remaining bags with openings to the left and place last bag with bottom flap facing toward front to create a neat back cover.

•Color-copy postcard. It could reflect an upcoming journey for you (or a friend if you are making a gift). Cut out image with deckle-edged scissors and adhere to top paper bag, 2" in from right side. Stamp a postmark and title beneath postcard: "bon voyage", "don't forget to write", or a personal message.

•Tie bags securely in a stack, placing ribbon 1" in from left spine. Using wire-edged ribbon will create a long-lasting bow. Secure with clothespins, being careful to capture ribbon at both front and back (old clothespins work best as their openings are slightly wider and flare at the tips).

VOYAGE

TRAVEL

I take a "travel bag" with me on every weekend jaunt. Mementos tuck into the front bag, which can later be included in the inside scrapbook pages. I sketch and take notes as I go along.

BON VOYAGE

Family Portraits

Materials

⅛" plywood boards:
    11" x 7", 4" x 6"
Assorted dimensional embellishments
Black acrylic paint
Family photographs
Old textbooks

Method

•Paint back and sides of large piece of plywood black. Allow to dry. Trim text to fit plywood and adhere with matte medium, pressing flat with brayer.

•Paint sides of smaller pieces of plywood black and allow to dry. Color copy your family photograph onto card stock or thick paper, enlarging to 4" x 6" if necessary. Trim with deckle-edged scissors and adhere to 4" x 6" piece of plywood with matte medium. Edges may extend slightly. Roll flat with brayer.

•Attach photograph board to background board with craft glue. Be certain to spread glue along all four edges. Press firmly. Lay flat and allow to dry overnight. Embellish with objects of your choice, attaching with craft glue or hot glue. Lay your piece down flat as you work; hot glue will dry quickly and allow you to plan your composition by looking at it standing up as well as lying down. I used elements that had a playful quality and maintained a sepia-like color palette.

•Display your family portraits by placing them on a small easel or line them up on a ledge.

No. 69—MULTIPLY

4
7
——
28

LA FAMILIA

A GAME

très petite

A KIND OF CANDY

Photographs languishing in old albums can be given a new life as an artful collection.

nonville
es Acacias. SAB. 26-00. Ouvert de mai à octobre. On
erdure, au bord d'un petit lac, une manière
u tout blanc qui connût une vogue fantas-
« Belle Époque ». Aujourd'hui, c'est fran-
lus calme, bien qu'on y organise toujours
ts, des garden-parties et de grandes récep-
riage. *

Altered Journal

Materials

Collage elements:
  Old letters, stencils, playing cards, wrapping
  paper, tickets, coupons, stamps, text,
  illustrations, paint chips
Gesso or acrylic paint, off-white
Grosgrain ribbon
Old book
Screw eyelet

Method

• Choose a book that is visually and
texturally appealing to you; one that you will
not mind altering. Open the book randomly and
apply gesso over the left- and right-hand pages
and allow to dry. If gesso is unavailable, a slightly
watered-down off-white acrylic paint can work
equally as well. Repeat this process approxi-
mately ten times throughout the book. Let the
text show through in some areas on each page.
Allow gesso to cure overnight.

• Continue this process until each page in the
book is coated with gesso.

• Approach the creation of your journal with a
free and open spirit. You may have a theme in
mind or merely want to gather your thoughts in
words and images. I tend to work intuitively and
therefore let elements flow and layer without a
lot of editing. This is a time to feel free and unre-
stricted by compositional "shoulds." Some of
your most creative touches will seem to appear
serendipitously. It is important to let the process
guide you and make bold choices when stuck.
Don't simply glue everything in place—attach
items with straight pins or clothespins. Paint over
areas you don't like, stamp a favorite quote vary-
ing letter size and font, tear a page out and tape
it back in sideways if it is really bothering you.

• Jot down notes as you go along. What you are
mulling over that day, secret dreams and aspira-
tions, or perhaps a sketch of your dog. Let your
words and images interplay naturally.

• I often address the cover last, so that if I want
to incorporate three-dimensional items, they
won't get crushed as I work in my book.
Rubbing a thin layer of paint onto cloth-bound
books works beautifully. Sometimes I will high-
light the title, other times I will create my own.

• Every book needs its own special bookmark.
Mine is a child's alphabet block that has been
covered with text, using matte medium. Attach a
small screw eyelet to the center of one side of
the block. Loop grosgrain ribbon, at least the
length of your book, through the eyelet and knot
to secure.

The Voice
of
The Big Firs

Altering books can satisfy a desire to give an old text new life as well as provide an inventive receptacle for your thoughts and scrapbooking needs. This project requires a time commitment and a willingness to enjoy the process as much or more than the final product.

UN FRUIT

A FRUIT

Another Idea . . .

Pass a book among your friends, allowing each to keep it for a week and add to it at leisure. Gather everyone for a viewing when complete.

REYNOLDS BROTHERS.

A. D. MORSE,
14th and Farnam Sts.

Inspiration . . .

UNITED
STATES
AIR
MAIL

Audubon 1785-1851

20¢

LITOGRAFICA
DOYEN · MARCHIS
TORIN

Patterns

Pattern for Paper Cones
on pages 30–31

Use pattern at 100% for 13" cone
Enlarge pattern 150% for 19" cone

A B C D E F G H I J K L M

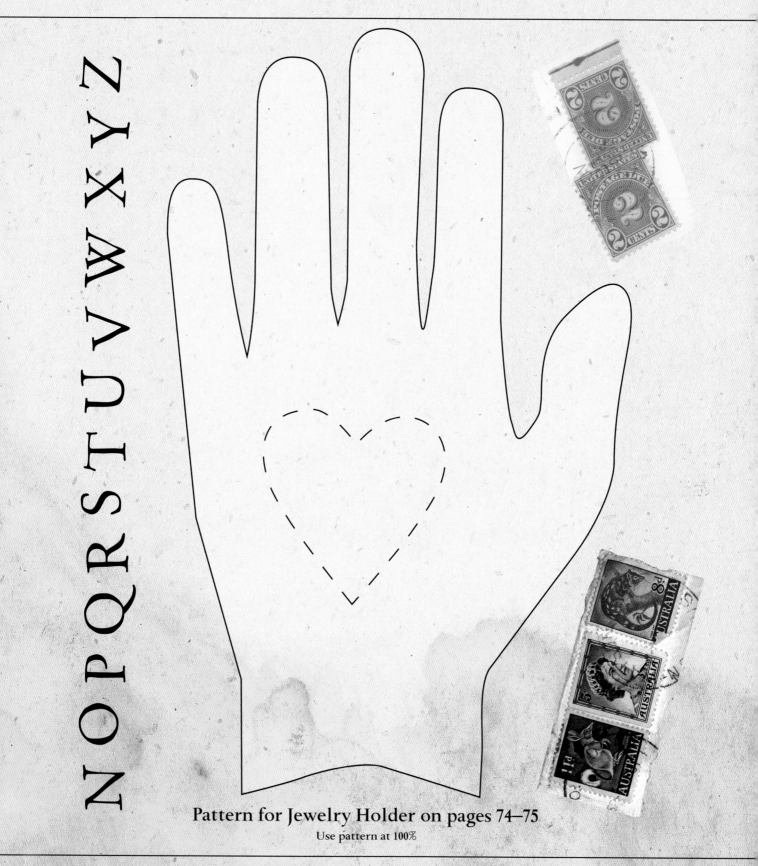

NOPQRSTUVWXYZ

Pattern for Jewelry Holder on pages 74–75

Use pattern at 100%

Artwork

Chapelle grants permission to consumer to make photocopies for personal use only.

AMORE

AMOUR

LOVE

LE COUSIN PONS

Le Cousin Pons, écrit en juin 1846, forme avec *La Cousine Bette*, dont il est inséparable, une sorte de diptyque : *Les Parents pauvres.* Balzac a expliqué l'idée commune des deux livres dans une lettre à Mme Hanska : « *Le Vieux Musicien*, — titre primitif du *Cousin Pons*, — est le *parent pauvre*, accablé d'humiliations, d'injures, plein de cœur, pardonnant tout et ne se vengeant que par des bienfaits. *La Cousine Bette* est *la parente pauvre*, accablée d'humiliations, d'injures, vivant dans l'intérieur de trois ou quatre familles, et y méditant la vengeance de ses froissements d'amour-propre et de ses vanités blessées ». Dans cette étude psychologique, la passion du collectionneur tient une place considérable ; Balzac était lui-même possédé par cette passion : la chasse chez les brocanteurs, la découverte d'un bibelot unique dans un bric-à-brac poussiéreux était une de ses grandes joies, et il avait rempli d'objets d'art le petit hôtel de la rue Fortunée qu'il avait acheté pour Mme Hanska, qu'il habita quelques mois avec elle et où il mourut. Dans *Choses vues*, Victor Hugo a décrit cet intérieur qu'il visita le jour même de la mort de Balzac.

UN PARASITE

Le Parasite est le titre que Balzac avait d'abord donné à son roman, qui s'appela aussi *Le Vieux Musicien*, avant de devenir *Le Cousin Pons.*

Sylvain Pons est un compositeur de musique, ancien prix de Rome, qui a eu à son heure de célébrité, mais qui, vieilli et oublié, vit péniblement en donnant des leçons de piano. De son séjour en Italie, il a rapporté l'amour des objets d'art, et sa passion de collectionneur, servie par un goût délicat et un flair subtil, lui a permis de réunir chez lui, à peu de frais, un véritable musée. Le cousin Pons, célibataire besogneux et gour-

MAYNIAL. — Le roman au XIXᵉ siècle.   10

HENRY ROWLANDS,
JEWELER & IMPORTER,
27 North Pearl Street,
ALBANY, N. Y.

UNITED
STATES
AIR
MAIL

Audubon 1785-1851

20¢

ČESKOSLOVENSKO
30
HALERŮ

—USE—
Lautz Bros. & Co's
PURE AND HEALTHY
SOAPS.
Try them! They are the Best Soaps in the Market.

The very best materials are used in the
manufacture of these Soaps.

HAPPY

FELIZ

THIS SPACE FOR WRITING MESSAGES

POST CARD

THIS SPACE FOR ADDRESS ONLY

PLACE STAMP HERE

DOMESTIC ONE CENT

FOREIGN TWO CENTS

LES BASSES-PYRÉNÉES

260. - OLORON. - LE PONT ET LE MOULIN

POST CARD

MESSAGE MAY BE WRITTEN ON THIS SIDE.   ADDRESS ONLY ON THIS SIDE.

Place the Stamp here
ONE CENT
For United States
and Island Possessions
Cuba, Canada and
Mexico.
TWO CENTS
For Foreign.

R-25763

Brookside Park, Dover, Pa.

autres qui ne sont pas commodes du tout, le tenaient si bien pour autre chose qu'un homme, qu'ils respectaient son pavillon en disant qu'y toucher c'était se frotter à Dieu. Il régnait sur le monde entier, tandis que 110 ceux-ci l'avaient mis à la porte de la France. Alors s'embarque sur la même coquille de noix d'Égypte[1], passe à la barbe des vaisseaux anglais, met le pied sur la France, la France le reconnaît, le sacré coucou[2] s'envole de clocher en clocher, toute la France crie : 115 « Vive l'Empereur ! » Et par ici l'enthousiasme pour cette merveille des siècles a été solide, le Dauphiné s'est très bien conduit[3] ; et j'ai été particulièrement satisfait de savoir qu'on y pleurait de joie en revoyant sa redingote grise. Le 1er mars, Napoléon débarque avec deux cents 120 hommes pour conquérir le royaume de France et de Navarre, qui le 20 mars était redevenu l'empire français. L'homme se trouvait ce jour-là dans Paris, ayant tout balayé, il avait repris sa chère France et ramassé ses troupiers en ne leur disant que deux mots : « Me voilà ! » 125 C'est le plus grand miracle qu'a fait Dieu ! Avant lui, jamais homme avait-il pris d'empire rien qu'en montrant son chapeau ? L'on croyait la France abattue ? Du tout. A la vue de l'aigle, une armée nationale se refait, et nous marchons tous à Waterloo[4]. Pour lors, 130 la garde meurt d'un seul coup. Napoléon au désespoir se jette trois fois au-devant des canons ennemis à la tête du reste, sans trouver la mort ! Nous avons vu ça, nous autres ! Voilà la bataille perdue. Le soir, l'empereur appelle ses vieux soldats, brûle dans un champ 135 plein de notre sang ses drapeaux et ses aigles ; ces pauvres

1. *la même coquille de noix d'Égypte,* en racontant la campagne d'Égypte, Goguelat a dit que l'Empereur revint « sur une coquille de noix, un petit navire de rien du tout qui s'appelait *La Fortune,* à la barbe de l'Angleterre. » — 2. *le sacré coucou,* l'aigle ; — autre transposition

familière de la proclamation. — 3. *le Dauphiné s'est très bien conduit,* à son retour de l'île d'Elbe (mars 1815), la marche de Napoléon, sur la route de Gap de Grenoble, à travers des populations ardemment patriotes, avait été triomphale. — 4. *Waterloo,* 18 juin 1815.

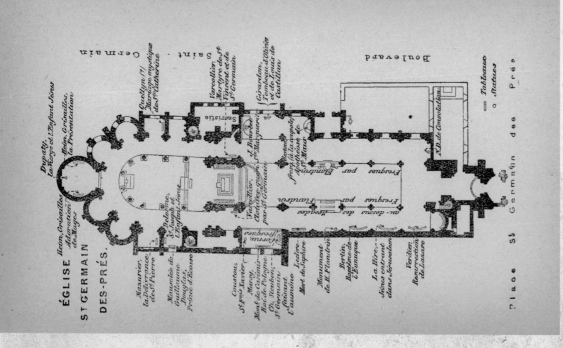

ÉGLISE
St-GERMAIN
DES-PRÉS.

Place St Germain des Prés

◻ = Tableau
○ = Statues

TRAVEL

Pennsylvania R. R. Bridge over Conestoga Creek, near Lancaster, Pa.

VOYAGE

PER VIA AEREA PAR AVION

Mod. 24-R

6
7
1
8
2
9
3
0
4
5

HENRY ROWLANDS,
JEWELER & SILVERSMITH,
Importer of
DIAMONDS,
WATCHES, CLOCKS,
Opera Glasses and Fancy Goods.
A Large Display of
Silver and Plated Ware.
NEW GOODS RECEIVED DAILY.
No. 27 North Pearl Street,
CORNER MAIDEN LANE
ALBANY, N. Y.

CANADA

CANADA

BINGO

62

B	I	N	G	O
4	16	36	51	61
13	26	41	52	72
9	29	FREE	47	63
5	18	44	55	70
2	25	38	46	74

MILTON BRADLEY COMPANY
"Makers of the World's Best Games"
Springfield, Massachusetts

A KIND OF CANDY

1946

À LA MAISON

BISTRO

CASA

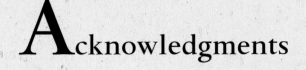

Acknowledgments

Thank you ... Thank you ...
•To Jo Packham for her confidence and tenacity, Lecia Monsen for her gentle guidance and Steve Aja for his good-natured patience.

•To Tracey and Molly for inspiration and blue moon nights.

•To my parents and Ken and Dave for instilling the belief that anything is possible.

•And to my husband, Nicolas for his unfailing interest, support and endless home-cooked dinners without which I would have subsisted on popcorn throughout this entire project.

Metric Conversion

mm-millimeters   cm-centimeters
inches to millimeters and centimeters

inches	mm	cm	inches	cm	inches	cm
⅛	3	0.3	9	22.9	30	76.2
¼	6	0.6	10	25.4	31	78.7
½	13	1.3	12	30.5	33	83.8
⅝	16	1.6	13	33.0	34	86.4
¾	19	1.9	14	35.6	35	88.9
⅞	22	2.2	15	38.1	36	91.4
1	25	2.5	16	40.6	37	94.0
1¼	32	3.2	17	43.2	38	96.5
1½	38	3.8	18	45.7	39	99.1
1¾	44	4.4	19	48.3	40	101.6
2	51	5.1	20	50.8	41	104.1
2½	64	6.4	21	53.3	42	106.7
3	76	7.6	22	55.9	43	109.2
3½	89	8.9	23	58.4	44	111.8
4	102	10.2	24	61.0	45	114.3
4½	114	11.4	25	63.5	46	116.8
5	127	12.7	26	66.0	47	119.4
6	152	15.2	27	68.6	48	121.9
7	178	17.8	28	71.1	49	124.5
8	203	20.3	29	73.7	50	127.0

Index

MH

DL 10-15-05

CR

MA

Corba, Anna.
Vintage paper crafts
33500008028839 (fo)
lqr

LAKE AGASSIZ REGIONAL LIBRARY
118 S. 5th St. Box 900
MOORHEAD, MINNESOTA 56561-0900